BEFORE THE FIRE

Genealogical Gleanings
from the

Cambridge

[Maryland]

Chronicle

1830–1855

Walter E. Arps, Jr.

WILLOW BEND BOOKS

2011

WILLOW BEND BOOKS
AN IMPRINT OF HERITAGE BOOKS, INC.

Books, CDs, and more—Worldwide

For our listing of thousands of titles see our website
at
www.HeritageBooks.com

Published 2011 by
HERITAGE BOOKS, INC.
Publishing Division
100 Railroad Ave. #104
Westminster, Maryland 21157

Other Heritage Books by Walter E. Arps, Jr.:

Before the Fire: Genealogical Gleanings from the Cambridge Chronicle, *1830–1855*

Departed This Life: Death Notices from The Baltimore Sun, *Volume 1: 1851–1853*

Departed This Life: Death Notices from The Baltimore Sun, *Volume 2: 1854–56*

Departed This Life: Death Notices from The Baltimore Sun, *Volume 4: 1859–60*

Heirs and Orphans: Anne Arundel County Distributions, 1788–1838

Maryland Mortalities, 1876–1915, from the (Baltimore) Sun Almanac

International Standard Book Numbers
Paperbound: 978-0-7884-3501-0
Clothbound: 978-0-7884-8659-3

INTRODUCTION

Rage sparked this book.

About 18 months ago I was hired by a Caroline Countian who wanted to join the D.A.R. To the best of this lady's knowledge, her ancestry was largely a lower Eastern Shore story involving the Gootee family of Dorchester and Caroline Counties.

In my search for a qualifying Revolutionary War ancestor, I quickly became mired in the Dorchester County impasse, stemming from the mid-19th century courthouse fire at Cambridge. Even the extraordinary contribution of Mr. James A. McAllister, Jr., in publishing his multivolume extracts of the saved land records helps the genealogist only so much.

The absence of Dorchester records led me to a roll of microfilm (M1073) housed at the Hall of Records here. This film contains disparate issues of the Cambridge Chronicle (established c. 1820) from 1830 through 1855 – but a woefully small number of issues given a 25-year timespan. The Hall of Records had obtained these Chronicles from F..... Malkus and Gary McNamara, the latter being an old Dorchester County surname.

While this microfilm did not actually further the cause of my client, who is still knocking on the D.A.R. door, it did introduce me to some Gootees I had not met before and whom I never encountered again. These precious newspapers also shed a bright beam of light on 19th-century Dorchester County life: its economic ups and downs, politics, Methodism, dependence on the steamboat, cultural aspirations.

A copy of this microfilm is also housed at the Dorchester County Public Library, which also houses some bound copies of the Chronicle for two years in the early 1920s. Between 1855 and the 1920s, no Dorchester County newspaper record appears to exist, and the Chronicle was not even published between 1855 and 1870.

Before my client terminated me for lack of progress, I had occasion, in Cambridge, to talk to Mr. Claude Gootee who, coincidentally, works for the Banner, a direct "descendant" of the Chronicle. I mentioned to Mr. Gootee that the Union List of Newspapers footnoted a cache of Chronicles as being in the possession, in the mid-1930s, of a Mrs. Shepard Bayly who was of Cambridge.

"I've heard that name," he said.

With a journalist's skill for detection, Mr. Gootee tracked down Mrs. Bayly's daughter in Rehobeth, Delaware, where this lady said that she had cartons of unlooked-at "stuff" that had belonged to her mother.

And she was not about to look at it, and I pulled out some more of my thinning hair.

So the possibility of a greater journalistic record of 19th-century Cambridge and Dorchester County remains open. Small wonder that, when Cambridge, my eyes automatically focus on the High Street attic line. I cannot help but wonder if there are not disintegrating copies of the early Chronicle to be found in the eaves of some of those proud houses.

What follows then are the gleanings I found in a comparatively few issues of the Chronicle. If you are interested, for example, in the Hurlock family, you will find paydirt here. As far as this researcher knows, this material represents the major bulk of genealogical assistance to be derived from the

Chronicle available in Maryland today. Some issues from the 1820s are to
be found at the Library of Congress, but none beyond 1840.

Good luck. The researcher of Dorchester County needs all possible assists.

                                              W. E. A., Jr.

Annapolis, March 15, 1978

Items From the Cambridge Chronicle

The following men are now serving as Judges of Elections in Dorchester County: District No. 1: Isaac Davis, Edward Wheatley, Francis B. C. Turpin; District No. 2: Robert Rawleigh, William Mobray, William Newton; District No. 3: Henry Wilcox, John T. Stewart, BEAUCHAMP ACKWORTH; District No. 4: Samuel Traverse (of M...), William Jones (carpenter), Hiram W. Woolford; District No. 5: George Mister, Asbury McNamara, Arthur H. Pritchett; District No. 6: Marcellus D. Keene, John W. Parker, Charles Traverse; District No. 7: Hooper Rawleigh, Peter LeCompte, Stanley Richardson; District No. 8: Charles Soward (sic), Michael Mitchell, and Thomas Applegarth. Saturday, Jun 1, 1844

Announcement is made of the current Dorchester County school commissioners: Fork: MINOS ADAMS, Isaac Davis, William Allen, John Collins, Samuel Twilley; New Market: James Thompson, Algernon Thomas, Henry W. Houston, William Mowbray, Mitchell Thompson; Vienna: Samuel S. Craft, James Gould, James W. Henry, James Donoho, G. W. Traverse; Parsons Creek: Reuben Tall, Joseph Brooks, Edward Harrington, John G. Bell, Traverse Spicer; Lakes: Benjamin G. Keene, George Mister, Henry L. McNamara, George Hart, Job T. Langrall; Hooper's Island: Benjamin Traverse, Charles Traverse, Samuel Creighton, Matthias Meekins, Samuel Dunnock; Comb: Anthony C. Thompson, John R. Keene, Thomas Wingate, John R. Creighton, Levin Mowbray; Neck: Peter Wheeler, William Frazier, Aaron Mitchell, Thomas Soward (sic), John Keene. William Creighton is treasurer of the Dorchester County primary school system at this time. Saturday, Jun 1, 1844

Married: On Tuesday last, by the Reverend William Dale, Mr. LEVIN ADKINS, to Miss Sally Hays, both of Dorchester County. Saturday, Oct 11, 1845

Deputy Sheriff WILLIAM H. AKERS announces that the lands of William Thompson, deceased, of East New Market, are to be sold in the near future. Sat, Sep 23, 1843

The property of John G. Andrews is to be sold in a Constable's sale. Mention is made in this announcement of Vincent Moore, Thomas E. Brown, and the firm of Clift & Williams. Sat, Feb 17, 1844

The land where Cain Insley and NATHANIEL ANDREWS now live is to be sold. Mary B. Lake and Henry L. McNamara are mentioned in this notice. Sat, Mar 16, 1844

In Cambridge, HENRY ANTHONY, ironworker, is now working in a shop opposite the establishment of Bell & Dail. Sat, Nov 1, 1845

Died - Lost overboard at sea, on October 15th, Captain Thomas J. APPLEGARTH, aged 35 years. Sat, Dec 6, 1845

Married: On the 1st inst., by the Reverend James M. Haines, the Reverend R... ATKINSON, of the Maryland Annual Conference of the Methodist Protestant Church, to Miss Olivia C. Newton, of Dorchester County. (Kent News please copy.). Sat, Sep 6, 1845

Mr. LUTHER BAIN is a candidate for the office of Sheriff of Dorchester County. Sat, Feb 17, 1844

Samuel Dunnock announces the forthcoming sale, to be conducted at John W. Traverse's store on Taylor's Island, of land there called Pleasant Grove, which formerly was owned by Mace Barnes and more recently by HENRY BARNES. Sat, May 24, 1845

Thomas Haywood, administrator of the estate of the late Mrs. HARRIET BARROW, asks that creditors submit their claims promptly. Sat, May 24, 1845

John F. Henry is admistrator of JOHN H. Barrow, late of Dorchester County, deceased. Sat, Apr 26, 1845

DANIEL W. BATES, Superintendent of the Cambridge Methodist Protestant Church Circuit, announces a forthcoming Camp Meeting, which is to be held at Tobacco Stick. Sat, Jul 26, 1845

In a letter to the Chronicle editor, Dr. ALEXANDER H. BAYLY denies the circulating rumor that he is treating a case of smallpox. This letter is followed by another, signed "Philanthropy," advocating the universal vaccination of Dorchester Countians. Sat, Jun 28, 1845

GARDINER BAYLY, Esq., is now serving as president of the Cambridge Henry Clay Club; James Dixon, Esq., its vice-president; and James Wallace, secretary of the Henry Clay Club. Sat, Jun 1, 1844

Mr. THOMAS BAYNE, of Oxford Neck, Talbot County, offers a ten-dollar reward for the return of a negro runaway named Charles Anderson, who is about 18 years of age and was raised near East New Market, Dorchester County. Sat Jun 1, 1844

Died - Of smallpox, near Bucktown, Captain JESSE BECKWITH, in the 29th year of his age (no death date provided). Sat, Dec 6, 1845

ARTHUR BELL, justice of the Dorchester County Orphans' Court, announces the release from debtors' prison of William Thompson, Eben Todd, and Job Ennalls. Sat, Dec 25, 1830

The forthcoming sale of the real estate of LEVIN BELL, deceased, is announced today. Sat, Dec 25, 1830

ROBERT BELL, Dorset Justice of the Peace, is occupying an office formerly occupied by Charles Corkran, adjoining the store run by Thomas Hayward. Sat, Jun 7, 1845

Married: in Dorchester County on the 14th ult., by Reverend Onins, Mr. WILLIAM BILLIPS, to Miss Mary Higgins, both of Dorset. Sat, Aug 2, 1845

JOHN BOUNDS, who resides near Quantico, Somerset County, offers a $150 reward for the return of his runaway negro named Cyrus. Sat, Dec 25, 1830

AMOS BOWDLE, treasurer of the Dorchester County public school system, advertises for a male primary-grade teacher to fill the vacancy at Brannock School House. Sat, May 24, 1845

In Chancery Court, the following relationships are established for HENRY BRADLEY, deceased: his widow, Sally Bradley; his sister, Sarah Bradley; Bat Murphy and William Murphy, sons of Peggy Murphy, a sister of Henry Bradley; Mary Chance, a daughter of Lucy Hicks, who is a sister of Henry Bradley; and the children of Nathan Bradley, a brother of Henry Bradley, whose names are unknown. Sat, Apr 13, 1844

Harriott Bradshaw is administrator of JACOB BRADSHAW, late of Dorchester County, deceased. Sat, May 18, 1844

JOHN BRADSHAW announces that he wishes to sell his 200-acre farm, two-storey house, large barn, corn houses, stables, etc., located on the county road leading from Vienna to Cambridge and within six miles of Cambridge and less than a mile from the Choptank River. Sat, Sep 23, 1843

Died - At his father's residence, on Tuesday last, 17th inst., JEREMIAH LAWRENCE BRAMBLE, in the 17th year of his age. Sat, Jun 21, 1845

Married: On Tuesday, the 16th inst., by Reverend Dr. ... Thompson, WILLIA BRANNOCK, to Miss Addaline Skinner. Sat, Dec 27, 1845

Married: On Thursday, 16th inst., by Reverend R... E... Kemp, Mr. WILLIS V. BRANNOCK, to Mrs. Rosanna B. Smith, all of Dorchester Count. Sat, Nov 25, 1843

THOMAS BREERWOOD, John W. Dail, and O. P. Hooper are identified as Justices of the Orphans' Court. James Wallace is identified, at the same time, as executor of James L. Wallace, Sr., deceased. Sat, Nov 18, 1843

John Brohawn is administrator of ELIZABETH BROHAWN, late of Dorchester County, deceased. Sat, Sep 6, 1845

Married: on July 23d, at Cabin Creek, by Reverend E. J. Way, Mr. Jabes L. BROHAWN, to Miss Mary E. Wright, both of Dorchester County. Sat, Jul 26, 1845

Trustee James A. Stewart announces forthcoming sale of nine properties of JOHN BROHAWN, situated at the mouth of Slaughter Creek. Sat, Mar 23, 1844

James Wallace is cited as trustee in a chancery case involving JOHN M. BROHAWN and others against James Brohawn et al. Sat, May 24, 1845

Married: on Wednesday, 6th inst., by Reverend M. D. Kurtz, Mr. W. Boaz, to Miss SUSAN MATILDA BROOKS, both of this county. Sat, Aug 23, 1845

Died - in this town, on Thursday last, Mr. ROBERT BURTON, at an advanced age. Sat, Aug 16, 1845

JOSEPH H. BYUS wishes to let a small farm at Town Point, situated on Fishing Creek and now occupied by Arthur Traverse. Sat, Nov 18, 1843

G. W. CALLAHAN, Esq., is editor and publisher of the Cambridge Chronicle. Sat, Dec 25, 1830

Daniel M. Henry, trustee, announces his intention of selling three wooded lots belonging to the heirs of LEVIN CAMPBELL, situated immediately on the road passing to the back of Appleby. Sat, Sep 6, 1845

Married: on Tuesday last, by Reverend M. D. Kurtz, Mr. THOMAS CARMINE, to Miss Teresa Clark, both of Dorchester County. Sat, May 24, 1845

Miss ___ CARROLL's Seminary for Young Ladies was opened in Cambrige, on Monday last. Sat, Apr 20, 1844

THOMAS D. CASE, is agent for the Choptank Steamboat Company; its steamer is named Cecil. Wed, Mar 14, 1845

CHARLES L. CHAPLAIN announces that a two-year-old Durham heifer, purchased from John H. Carroll, has strayed form his premises and asks the finder for its return. Sat, Jun 7, 1845

Died - in New Haven, Connecticut, on the 12th inst., Frances Chop(?)ard, infant daughter of EDWARD K. CHAPLAIN and Amenaide C. Chaplain, of Natchez, Mississippi, aged 12 months, 17 days. Sat, Aug 23, 1845

The Dorchester County Whig nominees for the Maryland House of Delegates are: Dr.(?) Joseph(?)Nichols,Dr. Francis P. Phelps, Levin Richardson and JAMES BOND CHAPLAIN. Sat, Sep 23, 1843

JACOB CHARLES announces an immediate opening for a teacher at the primary school at Federalsburg Sat, Nov 1, 1845

Mr. J. R. CODET, of Baltimore, announces that he intends to establish a dancing and waltzing academy in Cambridge and that he is prepared to instruct in the "new and beautiful La Polka." Sat, Apr 26, 1845

Married: on the 21st inst., by Reverend James M. Haines, Mr. FRANCIS COLLINS, to Miss Jane Bonner, both of this county. Sat, Sep 27, 1845

E. Richardson Hooper, trustee, wishes to sell the former WILLIAM COLSTON house, at Church Creek, which was once occupied by Reverend Harris and is presently being lived in by CHARLES CONNELLY. Sat, Mar 16, 1844

James Wallace, administrator of the estate of AARON COOK, deceased, announces that a negro woman and two negro girls are for sale. Sat, Jan 24, 1846

Married: on Sunday, 21st inst., Mr. JOHN COOK, to Miss Margaret Jane Seward, both of Dorset. Sat, Dec 27, 1845

THOMAS COOK and his wife Julia are the administrators of Prudence Traverse, late of Dorchester County, deceased. Sat, Sep 28, 1844

Mr. SAMUEL CORKRAN, of Cambridge, announces that he wishes to sell "a little farm" immediately on the Great Choptank River, at the mouth of Cabin Creek, which for several years was occupied by Mr. Ozburn. Sat, Sep 27, 1845

Departed this life, at his residence in Cambridge, SAMUEL CORKRAN, in the 62d year of his age. Sat, Jan 16, 1846

MR. JOEL CORNWELL, of Vienna, announces his intention of moving to Baltimore. Sat, Sep 6, 1845

Thomas Creighton, executor of ISAAC CREIGHTON, intends to sell the lands of William Dean (of George). Sat, Sep 27, 1845

B. H. CROCKETT is an apothecary, at Vienna. Sat, Sep 20, 1845

Died - on the 5th inst., Mrs. ELIZABETH DAIL, in the 66th year of her age. Wed, Mar 14, 1855

JOHN W. DAIL is president and Joseph H. Byus, secretary, of the Dorchester County Reform organization. Sat, Sep 6, 1845

WILLIAM B. DAIL, sheriff and collector, mentions the suit of Solomon Robinson and use of William Rea against the goods and chattels, lands, and tenements of Betsy Jackson. Sat, Sep 23, 1843

Dr. JOHN W. DASHIELE is now living and practicing in Virginia. Sat, Sep 23, 1843

Chancery sale of the property of GEORGE DAVIS: James Thompson, trustee, advises all persons having claims against the estate of Joseph Thompson, a negro who removed to Liberia, late of Dorchester County, to submit them. Sat, Nov 18, 1843

Married: by Reverend E. J. Way, Mr. JOHN W. DAWSON, to Miss Mary E. Newton, both of Dorset. Sat, Nov 1, 1845

MARTIN M. DEAN, who resides near East New Market, wishes to sell "Bachelor's Forrest" (277 acres), purchased from George Crosby, in Vienna District, near the lands of Alexander Sherman. Sat, Nov 15, 1845

The properties of WILLIAM DEAN are to be sold: "Pritchett's Forest,""Bramble's Meadow," and "Andrews' Fortune." Mention is made of Daniel Wrotten. Sat, Nov 1, 1845

ROBERT DILEHAY is administrator of the estate of JOHN DILEHAY, late of

Dorchester County, deceased. Sat, Jun 22, 1844

Amos Bowdle is administrator of the estate of NOAH DIXON, late of Dorchester County, deceased. Sat, Sep 28, 1844

The estate of Isaac Dunnock, late of Dorchester County, deceased is being administered by LEVIN DUNNOCK. Sat, Jun 22, 1844

The following men are Dorchester County Whig Delegate nominees for the Maryland Assembly: William Frazier, James Smith, who is of Somerset County, JOHN F. ECCLESTON, and Dr. John Boone; Sheriff: Kendall M. Jacobs; County Commissioners: Samuel Meekins and Barzilla Slacum. Sat, Aug 2 1845

JOSEPH ECCLESTON, Esq., is now editor and publisher of the Cambridge Chronicle. Sat, Sep 23, 1843

HENRY H. EDMONDSON, Sr., announces his removal to Dr. ... Rich's spacious brick house, in East New Market, which was formerly utilized as a tavern, where he is prepared to accommodate travellers and transient and permanent boarders. Sat, Dec 25, 1830

Married: On the 14th inst., by the Reverend R... E... Kemp, Mr. HENRY E. ELLIOTT, to Miss Emaline Marshall. Sat, May 18 1844

Married: On Tuesday, the 16th inst., by the Reverend Dr. ... Thompson, Mr. WILLIAM ELLIOTT, to Miss Mary Woolford. Sat, Dec 27, 1845

THOMAS ESGATE, of Church Creek, offers a six-cent reward for the return of a runaway white boy, Robert Alexander Welch, and indentured apprentice. Sat, Sep 30, 1843

Newly Appointed Dorset Justices of the Peace: Charles Smith, William L. Drura, Samuel Twilley, William Newton, Edwin R. Goslin, Edward W. Tull, Daniel Cannon, Jeremiah Bramble, George A. Z. Smith, William McMichael, Joel Cornwell, FISHER EVANS, Thomas S. Saxton, Isaac B. Cray, Henry C. Elbert, Whitefield Woolford, Algernon Thomas, Charles J. Smith, and Levin W. Stewart. Also William F. Geohegan, Traverse B. Tolley, James Smith (Somerset County), Henry Shenton, Solomon Foxwell, David W. Tyler, Clement McNamara, Charles Traverse, Fielder Jones, James Moore, James Mowbray, Jr., Richard Pattison, Henry Cook, William Rea, Edward Thomas, Samuel Abbott, Solomon Robinson, James Hammersly, Stanley Richardson, James Gould, John A. Radcliff, William Geohegan (of John), Samuel Craig, Thomas Jones, William T. Staplefort, and Stewart Keene. Also Richard Tall, James E. Goslin, Henry D. Wright, James Smith (of L.), Michael Charles, Elisha Corkran, John G. Abbott, Edward A. Marshall, Edward W. Morris, Edward Brodess, George W. Orem, John Brohawn (of William), John D. Stevens, Caleb Griffin, James Rea, Charles Corkran, Samuel Creighton, John E. Rozzell, and Samuel Griffin; Coroners: George W. Loockerman, Levin Wingate, Walter Kirby, Martin M. Dean, Isaac Millican, Caleb Mcnamara, and William D. Traverse. Sat, Apr 20, 1844

Mr. JOHN D. FARQUHARSON announces that he is quitting the business of farming. Sat, Oct 12, 1844

Married: By the Reverend M.D. Kurtz, Mr. BENJAMIN FITZHUGH, to Angeline Parker, both of Dorchester County. Sat, Nov 1, 1845

Announcement is made of the forthcoming Sheriff's sale of LEVIN FITZHUGH's farm. Mention is made in this announcement of the suits of Daniel Martin, Martin L. Wright, James Dixon, and John Staplefort. Sat, Dec 25, 1830

Thomas White, Josiah Bayly, S. D. LeCompte, Thomas Breerwood, SILAS FLEMING, B. D. Jackson, and James Rea comprise a committee, appointed by the Dorchester

Reform group, to ascertain the views of candidates for the Maryland Legislature on the subject of reform. The organization advocates revising the State Constitution so as to effect a wholescale system of reform, including lightened taxes, a diminished state debt, and "equal laws and equal rights" to be guaranteed to the people. Sat, Aug 16, 1845

THOMAS FLINT, of Cambridge, announces that he is now selling Wistar's Balsam of Wild Cherry, for a dollar a bottle. Sat, Feb 17, 1844

Sheriff's Sale: This item mentions the suit of David W. Corkran, whose wife Priscilla survives him, against the goods and chattels of ZEBEDEE FOXWELL, which are in the hands of Solomon Foxwell and Eliza his wife, administrators of the estate of Zebedee Foxwell. Sat, Jun 1, 1844

WILLIAM FRAZIER is administrator of the estate of Robert B. Spedden, deceased. Sat, Oct 18, 1845

Dr. HENRY FROST announces that he is now living at the head of the Choptank River, near Beckwith's Meeting House, Dorchester County. Sat, Sep 23, 1843

Married: On the 17th ult., by the Reverend Henry Slicer, Mr. GEORGE FULLER, formerly of Ware County, Georgia, and Miss Amelia Kelley, of Dorchester County. Sat, May 24, 1845

A Cambridge barber, THOMAS FULLER, advises that he is now stocking "shampoone." Sat, Apr 26, 1845

Constable George W. Wingate announces the upcoming sale of the lands of STEWART GEOHEGAN and William R. Robinson; Wingate mentions the suit of William Rea, administrator of the estate of Henry Page, late of Dorchester County, deceased. Sat, May 24, 1845

The suit of Rosey Traverse is mentioned in an advertisement, placed by Constable William R. Tall, of the forthcoming sale of the real estate of WILLIAM GEOHEGAN (of John). Sat, May 24, 1845

The Cambridge Literary Club announces an upcoming debate on the topic: Should imprisonment for debt be abolished? B.J. GOLDSBOROUGH and Mr. Corkran will argue pro; Messrs. Browne and Callahan, con. Sat, Dec 25, 1830

CHARLES GOLDSBOROUGH, commissioner, mentions in print today the late Thomas Meekins, of Dorset, and Mary Hutson. Wed, Mar 14 1855

Attorneys Joseph E. Muse, Jr., and NICHOLAS GOLDSBOROUGh announce that they are now occupying an office next door to that of Dr. Alexander H. Bayly, near the Cambridge Court House. Sat, Sep 30, 1843

N.L. Goldsborough, Esq., announces that he wishes to let an office which is situated next to the residence of Mrs. S. Y. GOLDSBOROUGH. Sat, Sep 30, 1843

WILLIAM T. GOLDSBOROUGH, advertising that he would like to sell a farm, on Fishing Creek, at Town Point Neck, states that it is currently occupied by Luther Bain. Sat, Apr 13, 1844

James Thompson is administrator of the estate of EBBEN GOOTEE, late of Dorchester County, deceased. Sat, Aug 30, 1845

WASHINGTON GOOTEE forewarns all persons from harboring or trusting his wife, Sarah Ann Gootee, who has left his bed and board. Sat, Feb 17, 1844

Married: By the Reverend R. E. Kemp, on Wednesday, the 8th inst., Mr. JAMES GORE, to Miss Elizabeth, daughter of Samuel Sewell, all of Dorchester County. Sat, Jan 16, 1846

The lands of Solomon Darby, deceased, are to be sold. Mention is made of JAMES GOULD, Landle & Serman, Marriott & Hardesty, William Rea (executor), and William S. Harper. Sat, Sep 23, 1843

ARCHIBALD GRAY is administrator of the estate of Matthias Willey, deceased. Sat, Jan 24, 1846

NATHANIEL E. GREENE announces that he is quitting Dorchester County and moving to Baltimore. Sat, Jun 7, 1845

Mr. CALEB GRIFFIN, of James Island, takes space in the Chronicle to announce that he wishes the rightful owner of a four-oared rowboad, which he found adrift and recovered, to claim it. Sat, Jun 22, 1844

Vegetable extract pills, which are said to cure anything from nervous disability to influenza, may be obtained from the following Dorset agents: White & Anderson (Cambridge), Muir & Wrightson (Hills Point Neck), SAMUEL GRIFFIN (Harescrable), William J. Vance (Hicksburg), Thomas J. Saxton (Big Mills), Samuel Corner (Neck District), Vickers & Handley (Vienna), Thomas K. Smith (East New Market), John L. Willis (Cabin Creek), Charles Connelley (Lower Hunting Creek), Jesse Hubbard (Upper Hunting Creek), John T. Stewart (Tobacco Stick), P.H. Graham (Golden Hill), Moses L. Keene (Slaughter Creek), William Mears (Draw Bridge), Brohawn & Morris (Crotchers Creek), and J. Bramble (Poplar Grove). Sat, Sep 23, 1843

Henry Page, trustee, for the disposition of EDWARD GRIFFITH's real estate, will resell, on Thursday, Jan 18, 1831, at McKnight's store house ... all that part of Edward Griffith's real estate, which was bid off in February last by Levin T. Fisher and Samuel Mo(w)bray. This property is being resold because of some misapprehension on the part of the purchasers.... It consists of one tract of land purchased by Edward Griffith from Henry Woodland and Lovey Brown, containing 87 1/2 acres.... The property also embraces another tract containing 208 acres, being part of Griffith's Attainment. The above land was bid off by Dr. Fisher. Sat, Dec 25, 1830

Mr. JAMES M. HAINES announces that he is running a bakery, in Cambridge. Saturday, April 26, 1845; James M. Haines & Company has a new cash store in operation, at Cambridge, stocking dry goods, boots and shoes, and groceries. Sat, Nov 29, 1845

At Cambridge THOMAS HARPER is selling "fashionable hats and caps." Sat, Nov 18, 1843

Married: On Wednesday evening (last?), by the Reverend Dr. Thompson, Mr. Thomas Harper, to Miss Elizabeth Ann Wingate. Sat, May 18, 1844

Married: In this town, on Wednesday morning, the 15th inst., by the Reverend James McKenny, WILLIAM E. HARRISON, Esq., to Miss Louisa N. Goldsborough, both of this county. Sat, May 18, 1844

THOMAS HAYWARD is the Cambridge agent of the Mutual Fire and Marine Insurance Company, of Baltimore. Sat, Sep 27, 1845

D. M. HENRY, attorney at law, is working out of an office in Cambridge opposite the store of the Messrs. Straughn Sat, Apr 20, 1844

Monsieur Guerand, a Franch fabric dyer, of Baltimore, announces that Mr. FRANCIS J. HENRY is his Cambridge agent. Sat, Jun 21, 1845; Baltimore dentist A. H. Briscoe announces that he will be in Cambridge for a week, for professional consultations, and cites these following Cambridge references: Dr. A. J. Thompson, N. L. Goldsborough, J. B. Lake, and Francis J. Henry. Sat, May 24, 1845; In the Saturday, Apr 13, 1844, issue of the Chronicle, it is announced that F. J. Henry has been appointed Cambridge postmaster.

Married: On Thursday evening last, by the Reverend James A. McKenny, Daniel Manydier, son of JOHN C. HENRY, Esq., of "Hambrooks," to Miss Henrietta Maria, youngest daughter of the late Honorable Charles Goldsborough, of Shoal Creek. Sat, Nov 22, 1845

JOHN F. HENRY, administrator of John Barrow, mentions Chancery suits of William Y. M. Edmondson, Nimrod Newton, and James Wallace. Sat, Mar 23, 1844

HOOPER C. HICKS announces that he as a large quantity of kersey and linsey, suitable for servants' wear, for sale. Sat, Nov 18, 1843; the suit of Hooper C. Hicks is cited in an item about the upcoming Constable's sale of the real estate of John Lee. Sat, May 24, 1845

THOMAS H. HICKS is identified as the Dorchester County Register of Wills. Sat, Sep 6, 1845

Died - At the residence of his uncle, JAMES HIGGINS, Esq., of Transquakin Mills (no age or death date provided). Sat, Oct 25, 1855

Died - At East New Market, on the 13th inst., Junius Alexander, son of THOMAS HIGGINS and his wife, Catharine Higgins, aged years, 10 months, and 11 days. On Tuesday, September 16th, Gilbert Motier, son of Thomas and Catharine Higgins, aged 6 years, 2 months; 17 days. Sat, Oct 25, 1845

JOHN H. HODSON is identified as the late Sheriff and Collector of Dorchester County. Sat, Sep 23, 1843; at a meeting of the Dorchester County Whigs, in Cambridge, on Tuesday, April 2d, John H. Hodson, Esq., was called to the chair, and J. Bond Chaplain was appointed secretary. The chair appointed Thomas H. Hicks, Jacob Willson, Henry Willcox, Robert Rawleigh, William Frazier, Samuel Harrington, Samuel I. Meekins, and James Cooper a committee to recommend to the meeting five suitable persons to represent the county at the upcoming gubernatorial convention. Sat, Apr 13, 1844

E. RICHARDSON HOOPER, of Vienna, who has been suggested for public office, announces that because of his age he is disinclined to reenter public life. Sat, Sep 23, 1843; the office of E. Richardson Hooper, attorney-at-law, is located opposite Mr. Bradshaw's Hotel, in Cambridge and Mr. Hooper is living in a room adjoining Mrs. Martin's residence, on Locust Street. Sat, May 18, 1844; the office of E. R. Hooper, Esquire, was robbed of $1350.00 on Sunday night by a person or persons unknown. Mr. Hooper is offering a $100.00 reward for the return of his funds. Sat, Jan 16 1846

JOSEPH S. HOOPER and Mrs. Anne E. Hooper advertise two wooded lots for sale, located on the road leading from Cambridge to Church Creek. Sat, Jun 1, 1844

Married: On Tuesday evening, the 28th ult., by the Reverend Edward Heffner, Mr. WILLIAM HOOPER, of Dorchester County, to Miss Amanda Stone, of Baltimore City. Sat, Nov 8, 1845

CHARLES W. HOPKINS announces that he is now operationg a cabinetmaking shop, next door to the business establishment of White & Anderson. Sat, Sep 23, 1843

Married: On Thursday, the 5th inst., by the Reverend John D. Onins, Mr. WILLIAM J. HOWARD, to Miss Joan Keene, all of this county. Sat, Sep 13, 1845

Married: On Sunday, the 21st., Mr. HENRY P. HUBBARD, to Miss Sarah Marshall. Sat, Dec 27, 1845

Married: On Tuesday, the 21st inst., by the Reverend W. Spry, Mr. THOMAS HUBBARD, Jr., to Miss Sarah E. Lecompte, both of this county. Sat, Nov 18, 1843

W. C. HUFFINGTON, of Big Mills, Dorchester County, announces that he wishes to rent the Tavern Stand, at East New Market, formerly occupied by Mr. D. Robertson. Sat, Sep 20 1845; William Huffington offers to let the buildings that were formerly occupied by Mary Ann Traverse, in East New Market, as well as "Tanyard," now occupied by William Turpin. Sat, Sep 6, 1845

DENWOOD HUGHES Solicits return of three head of cattle (marked), which strayed from Indian Bone Farm, near Bucktown. Sat, Nov 29, 1845

Departed this life, at his residence in Easton, Talbot County, on Sunday, the 7th inst., Colonel WILLIAM HUGHLETT, in the 77th year of his age. Sat, Dec 13, 1845

Married: On Thursday, the 12th inst., by the Reverend James M. Haines, Mr. JOSEPH HURLEY, to Miss Caroline Harvy (sic). Sat, Jun 14, 1845

Married: On Monday, the 1st inst., by the Reverend R. E. Kemp, at Mr. A. Hurley's home, Mr. MITCHELL HURLEY, to Miss Sarah Hurley, all of Hurley's Neck, Dorchester County. Sat, Sep 6, 1845

There is to be a Sheriff's sale of the property of JONATHAN HURLOCK and John Hurlock, including "Hurlock's Regulation" (217 acres), in the East New Market district. Mention is made of Edward W. Morris, Silas Collins, Cyrus Lord, and Nathan Vickars (executor of John Hurlock). Sat, Feb 17, 1844

JOHN HURLOCK is administrator of Levin Hurlock, late of Dorchester County, deceased. Sat, Jun 22, 1844

In Chancery: WILLIS HURLOCK v. Nancy Foxwell, William Hurlock and others. The bill states that Levin Hurlock hath departed this life intestate, seized of real estate in Dorchester County and leaving a certain Thomas Hurlock, his brother; a certain Sarah Cohee, his sister; a certain Nancy Foxwell, another sister; and James Hurlock, Jonathan Hurlock, John Hurlock, Eliza Thomas (wife of Thomas Thomas), Sophia Hurlock, and Sally Hurlock, children of a certain James Hurlock, which said James Hurlock was also a brother of said Levin Hurlock and who is now dead ... and the following grandchildren: James Hurlock, William Hurlock, Mary Jane Hurlock, and Delia Hurlock, children of Morton Hurlock (Morton, son of James Hurlock), also Sufkin Hurlock (son of Jere Hurlock); Jere, a brother of said Levin Hurlock. Also Diana Collins, daughter of Polly Noble (Polly Noble, sister of Levin Hurlock); also Rosa Phillips, wife of Elisha Phillips; and Eliza Hall, wife of Elsey Hall; and children of Phany Webb (said Phany sister of Levin Hurlock); also John Hurlock and William Hurlock, brothers of Levin Hurlock. Sat, Apr 13, 1844

STEPHEN HURST warns the general public against gunning, hunting, or seine hauling on the beach or premises of Weer Neck Farm and Tate's Bank. Sat, Feb 17, 1844

Joel Cornwell, administrator of ESAU INSLEY, late of Dorchester County, deceased, announces that three Negroes belonging to Insley are purchasable as of this date. Sat, Apr 5, 1845

JACOB INSLEY, of Vienna, announces that he recently took up an empty bateau, adrift near the middle of the Potomac River and nearly opposite Maryland Point, and wishes its rightful owner to claim it. Sat, Nov 18, 1843

A Sheriff's sale announcement includes mention of a suit of JOSEPH INSLEY for use of Caroline M. Insley and Isaac Andrews, against Clement McNamara, agent for George Meredith. Henry Bibby, deputy of the late Sheriff, will conduct the sale at the store of William Andrews, in Lakes District. Mention is made of Robinson's Neck, where mother of said Meredith now resides. Sat, Dec 27, 1845

THOMAS L. JACKSON is operating a new carriage shop, in Cambridge, adjacent to Dorchester House. Sat, Nov 18, 1843

WILLIAM JACKSON is administrator of the estate of Charles Leary, deceased. Sat, Feb 17, 1844

Mrs. WILLIAM JACKSON served as recording secretary of a spontaneous non-partisan meeting, held on Wednesday, the 25th inst., at the Cambridge Court House, triggered by the news of Andrew Jackson's death. Sat, Jun 28, 1845 (Ed. note: the former President died on Jun 8, 1845, and was buried at the Hermitage, in Nashville.)

KENDALL M. JACOBS, Esq., is a candidate for Dorchester County Sheriff. Sat, May 4, 1844

Died: On Friday, the 13th ult., at his residence at Fishing Creek, JOSHUA JEFFERSON, in the 50th year of his age. Baltimore Sun, American Whig, and National Intelligencer please copy. Sat, Oct 12, 1844

Samuel Pattison, W. Henry Pattison, Nehemiah LeCompte, John R. Pattison (W. Bridge), Samuel Hooper, Richard Jenkins, and HENRY JENKINS warn the citizens of Dorchester County not to hunt or otherwise trespass on their respective properties. Sat, Sep 28, 1844

Married: On the 14th inst., by the Reverend Daniel Davis, Mr. CHARLES W. JONES, of Virginia, to Miss Ellen Woolford, daughter of Whitefield Woolford, Esq., of this county. Sat, May 18, 1844

The following Dorchester Countians are serving as Trustees of the Poor: Minos Adams, John Pattison, John Vincent, Charles Tubman, Benjamin Woodard (sic), Reuben Tall, and FIELDER G. JONES. Sat, Jun 1, 1844

In an item about a new Henry Clay Club, at Church Creek, mention is made of Stanley Richardson, John R. Martin, John Dorsey, John Richardson, Dr. T. K. Carroll, George W. Jefferson, JOHN R. KEENE, Thomas Mace, John Woolford, A. W. Jones, and T. J. Christopher. Sat, Jun 1, 1844

Died - On the 21st ult., at the residence of her brother, in Baltimore, LETITIA KEENE, consort of John Keene, of Castle Haven, Dorchester County, in the 48th year of her age. Sat, Nov 1, 1845

Married - On Taylor's Island, on the 14th inst., by the Reverend Mr. Bayley, Mr. WILLIAM KEENE, of Baltimore, to Mrs. Susan A. Edmondson, of the former place. Sat, Nov 25, 1843

E. G. Kerr, Esq., of Easton, announces that he wishes to sell his farm called "Shoal Creek," situated two miles from Cambridge, as well as all of his lands in Caroline and Talbot Counties. Sat, Apr 26, 1845

James B. Steel, Jr., WILLIAM KIRBY, and Thomas M. Flint, of the Dorchester Troop, announces that the Cambridge Guards will march for an hour and a half on the 22d, commemorationg Washington's Birthday. Sat, Feb 17, 1844

SOLOMON KIRWAN is administrator of the estate of Philip H. Graham, deceased. Sat, Nov 29, 1845

The Reverend M. D. KURTZ announces that a Methodist Camp Meeting is to be held at Cherry Point. Sat, Aug 2, 1845

Died - On Friday, the 6th inst., at Church Creek, Mrs. SARAH ANN KURTZ, wife of the Reverend Michael D. Kurtz and daughter of Joseph Smithers, Esq., of Dover Delaware, in the 22d year of her age, leaving a daughter, the couple's only child. Sat, Sep 13, 1845

Married: On Thursday last, by the Reverend Dr. Thompson, GABRIEL P. LAKE, Esq., to Miss Henrietta Crawford, all of Dorchester County. Sat, Apr 5, 1845

ROBERT P. LAKE announces the forthcoming sale of land, at the store of John T. Staplefort, Lake's District, "McNamara's Property," situated on the Blackwater River; also the farm at the upper end of Hooper's Island, now occupied by the widow of the late Thomas Parks; as well as a property adjoining it, where Solomon Park now lives. Sat, Nov 8, 1845

THOMAS LAMBDEN is identified as administrator of the estates of Regby Lamden and James W. Palmer, both deceased and late of Dorchester County. Sat, Apr 13, 1844

Married: On the 30th ult., by the Reverend R. E. WILLIAM LAMBDEN, to Mrs. Jane Wolfe, formerly of Talbot County. Sat, Apr 5, 1845

JOSIAH LAYTON announces a Constable's sale, mentioning William McMichael, Kendal Fooks, William D. Barrow (administrator of John H. Barrow), George W. Traverse (administrator of John W. Twilley), John T. Stewart, William Mears, William Layton, Hooper C. Hicks, Richardson Gambriel, Jenkins Horseman, and R. Corkran. Mention is also made of the property of Stephen D. Ruark, Thomas H. Ruark, Horatio Hughes, Levin Woollea, Charles Johnson, and Josiah Webb. Sat, Nov 25, 1843

Mr. William K. Ackworth, Constable, announces the forthcoming sale of the real estate of THOMAS LAYTON; mention is made of the legal suit of Jacob Insley. Sat, May 24, 1845

Married: On Wednesday morning last, by the Reverend S. B. Southerland, the Reverend JAMES M. HAINES, of the Methodist Protestant Church, to Miss Esther Ann LeCompte, both of Cambridge. Sat, Nov 15 1845

Died - On Sunday morning last, Mr. JOHN S. LECOMPTE, in the 22d year of his age. Sat, Dec 6, 1845

Charles L. Chaplain, SAMUEL DEXTER LECOMPTE, and William A. Spencer are practicing attorneys in Cambridge. Sat, Sep 23, 1843; Judge Goldsborough and S. Dexter LeCompte are two of the speakers who will participate in the 69th observance of American Independence, on July 4th, at Church Creek. Sat, Jun 21, 1845

WILLIAM W. LECOMPTE, justice of the Peace, is to be found at an office in Cambridge, situated opposite the residence of Thomas White. Sat, May 24, 1845

JACOB LEVERTON, of Lower Hunting Creek, wishes to sell his grist and saw mills, two lots, two tenements, a blacksmith shop and his smith tools, it is announced today. Sat, Sep 23, 1843

The announcement of a forthcoming Chancery sale mentions Nancy Corkran and MARY LEWIS, as well as a deed dated 31 Jan 1824. Sat, Sep 23, 1843

WILLIAM C. LITTLETON, tailor, announces that his shop is situated on Race Street, in Cambridge, next door to the office occupied by John F. Henry, E and nearly opposite the store operated as Straughn & Company. Sat, Sep 23, 1843

James A. Stewart, Trustee, has been authorized to sell the real estate devised to Garrison McCollester to SAMUEL MCCOLLESTER "during his lifetime." Mr. Stewart also announces a forthcoming Chancery sale of valuable properties, situated at Town Point, called "Skinner's Conclusion" or "Fooks' Regulation" (197 acres), now occupied by Mr. William Fooks, on the Little Choptank River. Sat, Sep 23, 1843

Charles L. Chaplain, Trustee, announces an upcoming Chancery sale, at John Staplefort's store, Lakes District, of the property of JOHN MCCREADY -

"McCready's Cost" and "Fishing Point." Sat, Feb 17, 1844

HENRY L. MCNAMARA wishes to dispose of the land under the tenure of Messrs. Jonathan Mills and John Scott (539 acres); the house at High and Church Streets, Cambridge, occupied by Mr. Price, as a store and dwelling; the house and lot where Mr. Charles Rea lives, adjoining the above and lying between it and the Methodist Meeting House, on Church Street. Sat, Dec 25, 1830; Mr. John Martin is administrator of the estate of Henry L. McNamara, late of Dorchester County, deceased. James Cooper is identified as the surviving partner of the firm of McNamara & Cooper. Sat, Apr 26, 1845

Married: On the 17th inst., by the Reverend Dr. Thompson, Mr. JAMES H. MCNEAL, to Miss Elizabeth Baker, both of Talbot County. Sat, Apr 20, 1844

The Honorable RICHARD B. MAGRUDER, one of the associate jsutices of the 6th Judicial District, died suddenly on Monday morning, in the 57th year of his age. Sat, Feb 17, 1844

Married: On Wednesday last, at Taylor's Island, by the Reverend M. D. Kurtz, Mr. JOHN MAGUIRE, to Miss Susan Wilson. Sat, Nov 15, 1845

William A. Sulivane, O.S., announces a forthcoming assembly of the Dorchester Troop of Horse, at which the Court-Martial is to be convened, comprised of William H. Yates, George W. Traverse, Jeremiah C. Wright, Thomas Stewart, and WILLIAM T. MANNING. Sat, Apr 20, 1844

Died - At an advanced age, DANIEL MARTIN (no specific age or death date provided). Sat, Jul 26 1845

Married: At Baltimore, on the 9th ult., by the Reverend Mr. Reese, Mr. JOHN MARTIN, to Miss Rebecca E. Orem. Sat, Nov 1, 1845

URIAH MEDFORD announces a Constable's sale of Jefferson Hurlock's property, to be held at John Willis' store, at Cabin Creek. Mention is made of Elisha Corkran and Stephen Andrews. Sat, Feb 17 1844. The same Mr. Medford announces that he has attached a smut machine (wheat cleaner) to the Lower Cabin Creek Mills belonging to T. K. Smith, Esq. Sat, Nov 22, 1845

In Cambridge, the JAMES MITCHEL Company is manufacturing plain and figured carpets, samples of which may be viewed at the store of Messrs. White & Anderson. Sat, Sep 23, 1843

Mr. J. W. R. MITCHELL announces that the schooner Betsy Hamilton is now available for transporting grain from Vienna to Baltimore. Sat, Dec 25, 1830

SHADRACK MITCHELL wishes to sell the house and lot now occupied by John Abbott, Esq., as well as a small farm, near Cord Town, now occupied by Aaron G. Cook. Sat, Jun 7, 1845

LEVIN MOBRAY announces his intention of renting four farms: one now occupied by Mrs. Mary LeCompte, which is situated between the Big Mill and the Little Brick Mill; one at Blackwater, now occupied by Solomon Wilson; one now occupied by Josiah Stoakes and William Bestpitch; and one now occupied by Josiah Marshall. Sat, Jun 22, 1844; Levin Mobray, of Maple Dam Bridge, advertises for an overseer. Sat, Dec 6, 1845

The property of SAMUEL MOBRAY, of Lakes District, consisting of "Saturday's Work," "Middleton's Range," "Adventure," and "Foxwell's Venture," is to be sold. Mention is made of Caleb Woodwin, Andrew Flanagan, Samuel Trimble, John R. Martin, Mary D. Barnes, James Rea, Charles Corkran, and Robert F. Tubman. Sat, Mar 16, 1844

Married: By the Reverend R. E. Kemp, on Wednesday, the 24th ult., Mr. JOHN MOOR, to Miss Ann Moor. Sat, Jan 16, 1846

The announcement of the Sheriff's sale of the property of JOHN MOORE, whose widow is Mary Moore, mentions the entangling suit of Thomas Smith (q.v., where Smith's middle initial is given as K.). Sat, May 24, 1845

Mr. J. B. MURRAY announces that he is opening a school for young lades: English, Latin, and Greek, with a surcharge for instruction in French. Sat, Sep 23, 1843

SOPHIA MURRAY warns the public against trespassing on "Clifton." Sat, Dec 6, 1845

Mr. JOSEPH E. MUSE wishes to purchase undrawn ashes and is prepared to pay 9¢ a bushel. Sat, Dec 25, 1830; Mr. Muse announces that he wishes to lease, for a year or longer, the building now occupied by Mr. Austin, as a dwelling and store, at the corner of High and Poplar Streets. Sat, Sep 23, 1843; Mr. Muse wishes to lease out, in Cambridge, a large storeroom located under the Chronicle office. Sat, Nov 18 1843; Joseph E. Muse is executor of the estate of Richard Hughlett, deceased. Sat, Jan 22, 1846

Died - On the 26th inst., at the residence of her grandfather, in this place, JOSEPHINE MUSE, eldest daughter of Joseph E. Muse and Anne E. A. Muse, in the 4th year of her age. Sat, Nov 29, 1845

Died - In this town, on Sunday last, at the residence of his father, Dr. Joseph E. Muse, GEROGE EDWARD MUSE, Esq., in th 30th year of his age. Sat, Nov 22, 1845

JOSEPH E. MUSE, Jr. and Nicholas L. Goldsborough, trustees, announce that "Fairview," in Dorchester County, is on the market. Sat, Nov 18, 1843

Married: On the 3d inst., by the Reverend R. E. Kemp, Mr. HENRY MYERS, to Miss Sarah Wheeler. Sat, May 18, 1844

Married : On Tuesday last, by the Reverend M. D. Kemp, Mr. J. Thomas Travers, a Baltimore City merchant, and Miss Sarah Rebecca, second daughter of MOSES NAVEY, of Taylor's Island. Sat, Jun 14, 1845

Married: On the 8th inst., by the Reverend Dr. Thompson, Mr. WILLIAM NORMAN, to Miss Maria E. Hill, all of this county. Sat, Apr 20 1844

Married: On Thursday, the 18th inst., Mr. JOHN H. NORTH, to Miss Rebecca Soward. Sat, Dec 27, 1845

Thomas H. Hicks, Jeremiah C. Wright, William B. Dail, John Stewart, and JOHN D. ONINS are identified as subscribers for a proposed Methodist Episcopal Church, which would be built in Cambridge. Sat, Jun 21, 1845

In this issue of the Chronicle, JOHN M. OREM & Co., merchant tailors, take advertising space. Sat, May 24, 1845

THOMAS W. OVERLY, of Centreville, Queen Anne's County, announces that he will pay the highest market price for 50 to 100 likely Negroes, 10 to 25 years of age, of both sexes. Mr. Lowe, Mr. Overly's agent, may be contacted at the Easton Hotel. Sat, Dec 25, 1830

WILLIAM OZMAN Forbids anyone from gunning or otherwise trespassing on his farm or the one at Chancellor's Point. Sat, Dec 25, 1830

Married: On the 12th inst., Mr. Robert Burton, to Mrs. MARTHA PARKER. Sat, Sep 23, 1843

JOHN PARVIN, innkeeper, announces that he is now operationg the Dorchester House, formerly occupied by William H. Yates, Esq., Sat, Sep 23, 1843

Died - On Monday, the 20th inst., Mrs. AMELIA PATTISON, at the advenced age
of 73 years. Sat, Nov 25, 1843

JAMES PATTISON, of Unity Hill, wishes to sell the dwelling house and lot
presently occupied by Miss Eliza Waggaman. Sat, Jun 22, 1844

JEREMIAH L. PATTISON is administrator of the estate of William H. Pattison,
deceased. Sat, Nov 22, 1845

SAMUEL PATTISON forewarns all persons from hunting with gun or dog on his
farm and Windsmore Bridge. Sat, Nov 18, 1843

W. HENRY PATTISON wants to sell three valuable horses. Sat, Sep 20, 1845

James Wallace is identified as trustee in the advertisement of a forthcoming
Chancery sale of the real estate of WILLIAM PERRY (150 acres), which is
located near the land of Jeremiah Bramble and which formerly belonged to W.
W. Eccleston. The sale is to be held at the tavern operated by Mr. Silas
Collins, in East New Market. Sat, May 24, 1845

FRANCIS P. PHELPS, of Dorchester County, is serving as State Senator; his
term expires in 1850. Sat, Oct 12, 1844

Died - In Cambridge, on the 14th inst., Charles Elliott, infant son of ISAAC
PHILLIPS and his wife Mary Phillips, aged seven months and thirteen days.
Sat, Nov 18, 1843

Died - In the County, on August 29th, in the 82d year of her age, Mrs. Phillips,
consort of REUBEN PHILLIPS, a Methodist ... and mother of a large family.
Died - In this county on the 25th inst., Mr. Reuben Phillips, in the 77th
year of his age. Both Sat, Sep 30, 1843

REUBEN E. PHILLIPS is executor of Reuben Phillips, late of Dorchester County,
deceased. Sat, Apr 20, 1844

ALGERNON S. PIERCY, Esq., and Captain John Rowins are Reform candidates for
the next session of Maryland Legislature. Sat, Sep 13, 1845

Married: On the 5th inst., Captain JAMES PRITCHARD, of Caroline County, to
Miss Catharine Matthews, of Talbot County. Sat, Sep 23, 1843

Mr. E. R. Hooper announces a Trustee's sale of the property of EDWARD RAWLEIGH,
deceased, whose widow is Sarah Rawleigh and infant son is William Rawleigh.
Sat, Aug 2, 1845

Died - At her residence in Blackwater, on Monday, the 8th inst., Mrs. Leah L.,
consort of Mr. Levin Mobray and second daughter of HOOPER RAWLEIGH, esq., in
the 34th year of her age. Sat, Apr 27, 1844

WILLIAM REA isidentified as the administrator of the estate of the late
Colonel Henry Page. Sat, Sep 30, 1843

Died - On the 5th of December 1843, at the residence of his son Jacob, at
Round Prairie, Wabash County, Illinois, the Reverend CHARLES REED, in the
84th year of his age. Sat, Nov 24, 1844

Died - In Baltimore City, on the 19th inst., JAMES S. REYNOLDS, in the 54th
year of his age. Sat, Nov 29, 1845

Married: On the 14th inst., EDWARD RICHARDSON, to Miss Ann G. Richardson.
Sat, Sep 23, 1843

Messrs. JOHN RICHARDSON and Luther Bain are candidates for Dorchester County
Sheriff. Sat, May 11, 1844; John Richardson is announced as a candidate for
County Sheriff. Sat, Apr 26, 1845

Died - in this town, on Tuesday last, Mrs. REBECCA RICHARDSON, having nearly completed her 85th year of life. Sat, Aug 30, 1845

WILLIAM C. RIDGAWAY, having removed from Dorchester County, appoints James Houston, Esq., of Cambridge, to handle his local matters. Sat, Dec 25, 1830

James A. Stewart announces the forthcoming Chancery sale, at the store of John T. Stewart, in Tobacco Stick, of "Thompson's Range" (106 acres), conveyed to Joseph Stewart by John and HENRY ROBERTSON, at Button's Neck. Also "West-Phalia," "Chambers' Chance," and "Thompson's Desire" (317 acres) conveyed by Joseph Stewart to A. C. Thompson. Sat, Nov 18, 1843

Married: On the 14th inst., Mr. DAVID ROBINSON, to Miss Ann Berry. Sat, Sep 23, 1843

Sheriff's sale: Mention is made of the suit of Henry I. McNamara, admistrator of the estate of JOHN B. ROBINSON, against the goods and chattels, lands, and tenements of Joseph Insley and Shadrack Gootee, in Lakes District ("Griffith's Outlet," "Providence," "Nuner's Pasture Enlarged," and "Nuner's Discovery"). Sat, Sep 23, 1843

RHODA L. ROBINSON is administrator of the estate of Lovey McNamara. Sat, Nov 22, 1845

WILLIAM ROBINSON warns the public against trespassing on his lands in Robinson's Neck, Straits Neck, and Straits Hundred. Sat, Nov 22, 1845

ARCHIBALD ROSS announces the forthcoming Chancery sale of the Caroline County plantation, situated on the east side of the Choptank River, adjoining the lands of General Potter and Robert T. Keene. Sat, Mar 23, 1844

EDWARD ROSS, of Blackwater, writes to the editor of the Chronicle that he has been a long-time supporter of the policies of Andrew Jackson and Martin Van Buren. But Mr. Ross confesses that he has switched his allegiance to the Democratic Whigs, because of a ruined currency, the breakdown of the labour classes (in which the writer places himself), and the refusal of the Federal Government to distribute the proceeds of Public Lands sales among the States. As a result, Mr. Ross announces his determination to vote for Pratt, Clay, and Frelinghuysen, as well as all the rest of the Whig candidates. Sat, Jun 22, 1844; Thomas H. Hicks, Register of Wills in Dorchester County, announces that Algernon Hurley is administrator of Edward Ross, late of Dorchester County, deceased. Sat, Nov 18, 1843

The sale of the real estate of WILLIAM ROWENS, late of Dorchester County, deceased, is upcoming. Margaret Rowens is identified as the deceased's widow. William Rowens' heirs are Francis H. Rowens, James D. Rowens, and Mary Jane Rowens, who is now married to Thomas Meredith. Other heirs are Harriett Bell Rowens, William Rowens, and Margaret Ann Rowens. Jeremiah C. Wright became the owner of the deceased's real estate. Sat, Jun 22, 1844

JAMES P. RUSSELL is administrator of the estate of Daniel Layton, late of Dorchester County, deceased. Sat, Jun 21, 1845

Married: On Wednesday last, by the Reverend Dr. Thompson, Mr. JOHN W. RUSSELL, to Miss Nancy Wroten, all of this county. Sat, Jun 14, 1845

Married: On the 14th inst., by the Reverend R. E. Kemp, Mr. THOMAS J. SAXTON, to Mrs. Harriot H. Beckwith. Sat, May 18, 1844

Married: On August 27th, by the Reverend Dr. Thompson, Mr. THOMAS SEWARD, to Miss Cassey Phillips. Sat, Sep 23, 1843

Married: On Tuesday, the 9th inst., by the Reverend R. E. Kemp, Brittenham H. Robinson, to Miss Sarah Margaret, daughter of Captain GARRETTSON SEWELL, of Vienna. Sat, Sep 13, 1845

E. R. Hooper, Trustee, announces the forthcoming Chancery sale of the late JOHN SHEHEE's plantation, "Hansell," on the Nanticoke River. Sat, Apr 20, 1844

HENRY SHENTON is identified as keeper of the Hooper Straights' light boat. Sat, Sep 20, 1845

Died - In this town, on Monday evening last, Mrs. Eliza, consort of Mr. CALEB SHEPARD. Sat, Sep 6, 1845

Mr. EBBEN L. SHORT is executor of the will of William Short, late of Dorchester County, deceased. Sat, Aug 23, 1845

In this issue of the Chronicle, BARZILLA SLACUM is announced as a candidate for Sheriff of Dorchester County. Sat, Oct 11, 1845

The Chronicle editor announces that he has been authorized to reveal that JAMES S. SLAUGHTER, Esq., is a candidate for a seat in the Maryland House of Delegates. Sat, Sep 23, 1843

JAMES T. SMITH, of East New Market, advertises wood for sale. Sat, Sep 30, 1843; James T. Smith is administrator of the estate of Levin Smith, deceased. Sat, Feb 17, 1844

In an item about a forthcoming Sheriff's sale of the property of John N. Moore, whose widow is Mary Moore, mention is made of the entangling suit of THOMAS K. SMITH. Sat, Jun 7, 1845

Dr. E. F. SMITHERS announces that he is now practicing in Vienna, out of an office in the residence of Mr. Crockett. Sat, Jun 7, 1845

Married: On Thursday, the 6th inst., by the Reverend John D. Onins, Mr. Robert B. Spedden, to Miss EMILY A. SPEDDEN, both of Dorchester County. Sat, Nov 22, 1845

Married: On the 20th of April, by the Reverend L. A. Collins, Mr. WILLIAM SANDERS, to Miss Angeline Christopher, both of this county. Sat, Apr 27, 1844

ROBERT B. SPEDDEN wishes to sell his windmill. Sat, Dec 25, 1830

Mr. S. W. LeCompte has placed the house lately occupied by Colonel THOMAS STANFORD on the market. Wed, Mar 14, 1855

Died - On Tuesday, the 12th inst., Mrs. ELIZA STAPLEFORT, wife of William T. Staplefort, Esq., and second daughter of John Crawford and his wife, Ann Crawford. Feb 17, 1844; Died - At Church Creek, William T. Staplefort (no age or death date provided). Sat, Jul 26, 1845; William W. Crawford, administrator of the estate of William T. Staplefort, late of Dorchester County, deceased, intends to sell the Staplefort property at Church Creek; it includes the schooners Eliza and Oceola. Sat, Aug 16, 1845

Mr. H. I. STARK, watchmaker and agent for William Galloway, of New York, announces that he will supply county storekeepers with hardware and other items, at the very lowest wholesale prices. Sat, Dec 25, 1830

The Reverend K. J. Stewart cites JAMES B. STEELE, Esq., of Dorchester County, as a reference in the advertisement of his English and Classical Institute, situated at Wilmington, Delaware. Sat, Jun 21, 1845; James A. Steele, Thomas Hayward, and Dr. Phelps give concurring reports, at a meeting of the Dorchester Farmers' Club, on the superiority of German wheat, now being grown in some parts of the County. Sat, Jun 14, 1845

Married: At "Lyford," near Denton, on the 4th inst., by the Reverend E. Bayley, Mr. JAMES B. STEELE, JR., Esq., to Miss E. G. P. Richardson, daughter of the late Joseph P. W. Richardson, Esq., of Caroline County. Sat, Nov 15, 1845

Married: On Tuesday, the 7th inst., by the Reverend R. E. Kemp, Mr. EDWARD STEPHENS, to Miss Elizabeth Ann, daughter of Henry Hicks. Sat, Jan 16, 1846

THOMAS B. SHERMAN, of "Waterloo," Indian Creek, advertises that his schooner Venus is available to transport Dorchester County produce to Baltimore City. Sat, Sep 28, 1844

JAMES A. STEWART is identified as secretary of the Dorchester County Farmer's Club. Sat, Apr 26, 1845; Died - James A. Stewart, infant son of James A. Stewart and his wife, Rebecca S. Stewart, aged eight months. Sat, Aug 16, 1845

Married: On Wednesday last, by the Reverend J. A. McKenny, THOMAS R. STEWART, Esq., of Chestertown, Kent County, to Miss Anna Maria James, of this place. Sat, Nov 15, 1845

William Rea, clerk of the County Commissioners, posts a reward of $20.00 for the apprehension of the arsonist(s), who set fire, on the 13th inst., to the premises of Messrs. JOHN T. STEWART and Thomas M. Flint. Sat, May 24, 1845.

EDWARD STREET announces that, via Philadelphia, he has just received the latest London and Paris style books and is preparted to cut out and make up all designs of gentlemen's apparel. Sat, Nov 18, 1843

HENRY J. STRANDBERG announces that he is now operating a bakery, confectionary, and fancy store, in the corner building, next to the printing office. Sat, May 18, 1844

Married: On Tuesday, the 7th inst., by the Reverend R. E. Kemp, Mr. SYLVESTER SULIVANE, to Miss Delsah Hurley. Sat, Jan 16, 1846

Married: On the 2d inst., by the Reverend James M. Haines, Mr. GEORGE SULLI-VAN, to Mrs. Sarah Horsman, both of Dorset. Sat, Sep 6, 1845

Died - At Tobacco Stick, on the 27th ult., DANIEL JOSEPH TALL (no age provided). Sat, Oct 11, 1845

REUBEN TALL, Sheriff, announces the fortncoming property sale, to be conduct-ed at the store of James Muir, of lands formerly belonging to Thomas Lee. Mr. Tall mentions Bartholomew Byus and Susanna Skinner. Sat, Dec 25, 1830

WILLIAM R. TALL is administrator of the estate of Job Trigoe, late of Dor-chester County, deceased. Sat, Jun 22, 1844

LEMUEL G. TAYLOR announces that the steamboat will, until the Spring, call at Castle Haven, on her route between Easton and Baltimore. Passage from Castle Haven to Baltimore costs $2.50, which includes dinner afloat. Sat, Dec 25, 1830

Died - In this county, near Cabin Creek, on Friday, the 17th inst., Mr. HENRY THOMAS, at an advanced (but otherwise unspecified) age. Sat, Dec 25, 1830

In the announcement of a forthcoming Sheriff's sale, mention is made of the lands of HUGH THOMAS ("James' Point"); Edward Thomas, Esq., and the ongoing suit of Richard Patterson are also mentioned. Sat, Sep 30, 1843

Mr. Ricksom Webb, of Caroline County, offers a $5.00 reward for the return of a runaway Negro boy named Alfred (no age provided), who formerly belonged to Dr. ABSALOM THOMPSON, of Dorchester County. Sat, Apr 27, 1844

Mr. A. C. THOMPSON is operationg a drug and medicine store now, at Cambridge. Sat, Dec 25, 1830; Mr. A. C. Thompson places his "beautiful little farm," called "Bellefield," adjoining Cambridge, on the market. Sat, May 4, 1844

JAMES THOMPSON announces thta he has upwards of 60,000 bricks for sale, near Vienna, which Mr. Horace Hicks is prepared to deliver to purchasers. Sat, Dec 25, 1830

JOHN THOMPSON, Samuel Sewell, Algernon Thomas, and Captain William Mears (Nanticoke) are candidates for the office of Dorchester County Commissioner. Sat, Sep 23, 1843

The lands of the late WILLIAM THOMPSON, Sr., are to be sold. Mention is made today of Charles J. Smith, William W. M. Edmondson, Thomas Baltzell and P. Baltzell. Sat, Sep 23, 1843

S. Mitchell, T. B. TOLLEY, E. Tall, and W. Woolford, Dorchester County school Commissioners, announce the opening of a new school near Church Creek. Sat, Dec 13, 1846

Died - On Taylor's Island, on the 4th inst., LEVI D. TRAVERS, in the 47th year of his age. Sat, Feb 17, 1844

DEVEREUX TRAVERSE announces the upcoming sale of land, bordering the Great Choptank River, in Talbot County, near the residence of William Hughlett, Esq., known as the "Cannon Farm." Sat, May 18, 1844

WILLIAM K. TRAVERSE, of Taylor's Island, advertises today that he would like the owner of the schooner Susquehanna (out of Baltimore), which was wrecked opposite his home about September 10, to remove it appurtenances. Sat, Oct 25, 1845

B. G. TUBMAN, Esq., is now editor and proprietor of the Cambridge Chronicle, which has switched its day of publication from Saturday to Wednesday. Wed, Mar 14, 1855

Married: In Baltimore City, on Tuesday last, Mr. RICHARD TUBMAN, to Miss R. Ann Stewart. Sat, Nov 15, 1845.

ROBERT F. TUBMAN, of "Glasgow," Dorchester County, announces that he wishes to sell the medical stand that his father used during his 32-year medical practice. Wed, Mar 14, 1855; Mr. Robert F. Tubman asks that hunters refrain from trespassing on his farm, situated on the northeast main road leading from Cambridge to Sandy Hill. Sat, Nov 22, 1845

Married: On the 2d inst., by the Reverend Dr. Thompson, Mr. GEORGE TWILLEY, to Miss Priscilla Williams. Sat, Jun 14, 1845

C. K. VEASEY, Esq., attorney, has relocated, in Cambridge, in an office next door to Mr. Hayward's store. Sat, Sep 23, 1843

Ordered in Chancery Court that the sale of the property in the case of PETER VICKERS against Isaac Wright and others, made and reported by Trustee James A. Stewart, be ratified and confirmed. Sat, Sep 23, 1843

STEWART VICKERS is acting administrator of the estate of Robert Clark, late of Dorchester County, deceased. Sat, Jun 1, 1844

JOHN VINCENT is administrator of the estate of Thomas Bendle, late of Dorchester County, deceased. Sat, Sep 6, 1845

There is to be a Chancery sale of ROBERT WALKER's property, which was purchased from John Newman, at Cabin Creek (300 acres). Sat, Feb 17, 1844

Married: In Baltimore City, by the Reverend William Dale, Mr. MARTIN L. WALL, to Miss Elizabeth Dean, both of Dorchester County. Sat, Oct 11, 1845

Married: On the 15th inst., by the Reverend Mr. Spry, Mr. ANTHONY R. WALLACE, to Miss Mary R. Applegarth. Sat, Nov 24, 1844; Anthony R. Wallace is administrator of the estate of George Howard, deceased. Sat, Dec 27, 1845

JAMES WALLACE announces the forthcoming private sale of the small farm where Samuel Abbot now lives, situated between Cambridge, on the road leading to the Bayshore and adjacent to the lands of Samuel Corner, and near Beckwith's Meeting House. Sat, Sep 23, 1843; James Wallace, attorney, is practicing now, in Cambridge, in an office adjoining the store operated by Henry & Hicks. Sat, Sep 23, 1843; James Wallace is corresponding secretary of the Dorchester County Temperance Society. Sat, Jun 1, 1844

Died - On Tuesday, the 27th ult., at his residence, near Ennalls' Camp Ground, WILLIAM WEBB, in the 45th year of his age. Sat, Jun 7, 1845

In the announcement of a Sheriff's sale of the property of ALFRED WHEATLEY, mention is made of Smith & Conaway, James Jones, Saul Briley, Thomas Brily (sic), and E. W. Morris. Sat, Mar 16, 1844

William Rea is authorized by the trustees of the Methodist Episcopal Church, of Cambridge, to sell the old church (33' x 36'), located on Church Street. The structure will be available for purchase as soon as the new church, on Race Street, is completed. Mr. Rea will also sell the back part of the lot on which the new church is now being constructed, fronting on Pine Street and running from thence to the back line of the lot sold by the trustees of THOMAS WHITE, Esq. Sat, Nov 22, 1845

Married: On Tuesday, the 16th inst., by the Reverend William Davis, Mr. WILLIAM WHITE, to Miss Lucia Conley, both of Dorchester County. Sat, Jul 26, 1845

H. WILLCOX, president of the Nanticoke Bridge Company, announces an upcoming directors' meeting, which is to be held at the Vienna tollhouse. Sat, May 24, 1845

Mr. CHARLES WILLIGMAN, now residing in Cambridge, offers a $50,000 (!) reward for "likely" Negroes, who can be sold in the New Orleans slave market. Sat, Sep 20, 1845

Announcement of a Sheriff's sale cites the suit of JACOB WILSON and the lands and tenements of Charles Calaway, in Fork District ("Hog Yard" and "Mahan's Chance"). Sat, Sep 23, 1843; Jacob Wilson is executor of the estate of William H. Akers, late of Dorchester County, deceased. Sat, Jun 21, 1845; John W. Dail is a major, Extra Battalion of Maryland Militia; John H. Hodson is a colonel, 11th Regiment of Maryland Militia; Josel Cornwell, lieutenant-colonel; Jacob Wilson, major; Henry Wilcox, adjutant; Joseph Brooks, colonel, 48th Regiment of Maryland Militia; Levin W. Stewart, lieutenant-colonel; Goodman Gootee, major. These Dorchester County military appointments have been made by the Governor, by and with the advice and consent of the Maryland Senate. Sat, Mar 23, 1844

GEORGE W. WINGATE announces a Constable's sale of the property of Stewart Geohegan. Mention is made of John G. Abbott, Charles Corkran, and William Rea (adimistrator of Henry Page.) Sat, Feb 17, 1844

WILLIAM WINGATE asks that his creditors submit their financial obligations. Sat, Feb 17, 1844

WILLIAM L. WINGATE, secretary, announces that members of Cambridge Lodge No. 66 will a funeral procession on behalf of their deceased brother, the Honor able John L. Kerr. Sat, Apr 13, 1844

Married: On Monday evening, the 10th inst., by the Reverend Edward Heffner, Mr. Levin Wingate, of Dorchester County, to Miss Margaret Elson, of Baltimore City. Sat, Nov 15, 1845

At Cambridge, Dr. WILLIAM WINGATE is now practicing in the office where
Thomas Woolford once practiced. Sat, Apr 5, 1845

HARRISON WINTERBOTTOM announces that he has opened a boot and shoe factory in
Cambridge, located near Mrs. Bradshaw's tavern. Sat, Dec 25, 1830

GEORGE WINTROPE wishes to rent a farm situated on the Transquakin River,
called "Buck Neck." Mr. Wintrope's real estate agent, in Cambridge, is Mrs.
Eliza Hooper. Sat, Jul 26, 1845

STEVENS B. B. WOOLFORD is executor of the estate of Stevens B. Woolford, late
of Dorchester County, deceased. Sat, Jun 22, 1844

Samuel D. LeCompte and WHITEFIELD WOOLFORD are Reform candidates for the
Maryland State Legislature. Sat, Sep 6, 1845

Died - In Baltimore, on the 19th inst., Ann Rebecca, wife of JAMES N. WRIGHT,
in the 27th year of her age. Sat, Nov 29, 1845

Married: (No date), by the Reverend R. E. Kemp, Mr. Thomas Corkran, of
Caroline County, to Hester Ann, daughter of KENNERLY WRIGHT, Esq., of Dorchester County. Sat, Aug 30, 1845

JOHN L. WRIGHTSON, administrator of the estate of Joshua Wrightson, announces
the forthcoming sale, to be held at B. H. Crockett's Hotel at Vienna, of a lot
in Vienna, which Thomas Byrn, in his lifetime, sold to Mrs. Margaret W.
Wright, being formerly owned by Samuel Hitchens, deceased. Sat, Nov 18, 1843

WILLIAM H. YATES announces his removal to a house known as the Masonic Hotel
which, for many years, was occupied by the late William Flint. Mr. Yates
anticipates entertaining travelers. Sat, Sep 23, 1843

INDEX

ELBERT Henry C. 5
ELSON Margaret 19
ENNALLS Job 2

FISHER Levin T. 7
FLANAGAN Andrew 12
FLINT Thomas M. 10, 17; William 20
FOOKS Kendal 11; William 11
FOXWELL Eliza 6; Nancy 9; Solomon
5, 6
FRAZIER William 1, 5, 8

GALLOWAY William (of New York) 16
GAMBRIEL Richardson 11
GEOHEGAN Stewart 19; W. (of John) 5;
William F. 5
GOLDSBOROUGH Judge 11; B. J. 6;
Charles 8; Henrietta Maria 7; Louisa
N. 7; N. L. 6, 7; Nicholas L. 13
GOOTEE Goodman 19; Sarah 6; Shadrack
15
GOSLIN Edwin R. 5; James E. 5
GOULD James 1, 5
GRAHAM P. H. 7; Philip H. 10
GUERAND Monsieur 7

HAINES James M. & Co 7
HAINES The Reverend James M. 1, 4, 9,
17
HALL Eliza 9; Elsey 9
HAMMERSLEY James 5
HANDLEY (See VICKERS)
HARDESTY (See MARRIOTT)
HARPER Thomas 7; William S. 6
HARRINGTON Edward 1; Samuel 8
HARRIS The Reverend 4
HART George 1
HARVY Caroline 9
HAYS Sally 1
HAYWARD Mr. (storekeeper) 18: Thomas
2(twice), 16
HENRY & HICKS 19
HENRY D. M. 7; Daniel Manydier 3, 7;
Francis J. 7; James W. 1; John F. 1,
11
HICKS (Also see HENRY); Elizabeth
Ann 17; Henry 17; Hooper C. 8, 11;
Horace 17; Lucy 2; Thomas H. 8, 13,
15
HIGGINS Catharine 8; Gilbert Motier
8; Junius Alexander 8
HILL Maria E. 13
HITCHENS Samuel 20
HODSON John H. 8, 19

HOOPER E. Richardson 4, 8(twice), 14,
16; Mrs. Eliza 20; O. P. 3; Samuel 10
HORSEMAN Jenkins 11
HORSMAN Sarah 17
HOUSTON Henry W. 1; James 15
HOWARD George 18
HUBBARD Jesse 7
HUFFINGTON William 8
HUGHES Horatio 11
HUGHLETT Richard 13; William 18
HURLEY Mr. A. 9; Algernon 15; Sarah 9
HURLOCK Delia 9; Delsah 17; James 9;
Jere 9; John 9(twice); Levin 9; Mary
Jane 9; Morton 9; Sophia 9; Sufkin 9;
Thomas 9; William 9
HUTSON Mary 6

INSLEY Cain 1; Caroline M. 9; Jacob
11; Joseph 15

JACKSON B. D. 5; Betsy 4
JACOBS Kendall M. 5
JAMES Anna Maria 17
JEFFERSON George W. 10
JENKINS Richard 10
JOHNSON Charles 11
JONES A. W. 10; Fielder 5; James 19;
Thomas 5; William 1

KEENE Benjamin G. 1; Joan ; John 1,
10; John R. 9; Marcellus D. 1; Moses L.
1; Moses L. 7; Robert T. 6; Stewart 5
KELLEY Amelia 6
KEMP The Reverend R. E. 3, 5, 6, 9, 12,
13(twice), 15(twice), 17(twice), 20
KERR E. G. 10; John L. 19
KIRBY Walter 5
KURTZ The Reverend M. D. 3(twice),
10(twice), 12

LAKE J. B. 7; Mary B. 1
LANDLE & SERMAN 6
LANGRALL Job T. 1
LAYTON DRniel 15; William 11
LEARY Charles 10
LECOMPTE Mrs. Mary 12; Nehemiah 10;
Peter 1; S. Dexter 5, 11, 20; S. W. 16;
Sarah E. 8
LEE John 8; Thomas 17
LOOCKERMAN George W. 5
LORD Cyrus 9
LOWE Mr. 13

MACE Thomas 10
MCCOLLESTER Garrison 11

3; Thomas 13; Thomas K. 7, 12
SMITHERS Joseph (of Dover, Delaware) 10
SOUTHERLAND The Reverend S. B. 11
SOWARD Charles 1; Rebecca 13; Thomas 1
SPEDDEN Robert B. 6, 16
SPENCER William A. 11
SPICER Traverse 1
SPRY The Reverend Mr. 18; The Reverend W. 8
STAPLEFORT John 5, 11; John T. 11; William T. 5, 16
STEELE James A. 16; James B., Jr. 10
STEVENS John D. 5
STEWART James A. (infant) 17; James A. 3, 11, 15, 18; John 13; John T. 1, 7, 11, 15; Joseph 15; The Reverend K. J. (of Wilmington, Delaware) 16; Levin W. 5, 19; R. Ann 18; Mrs. Rebecca S. 17; Thomas 12
STOAKES Josiah 12
STONE Amanda 8
STRAUGHN Messrs. 7
STRAUGHN & CO. 11
SULIVANE William A. 12

TALL E. 18; Reuben 1, 10; Richard 5; (Constable) William R. 6
THOMAS Algernon 1, 5, 18; Edward 5, 17; Eliza 9; Thomas 9
THOMPSON Dr. 10; The Reverend Dr. 3, 5, 7, 12, 13, 15(twice), 18; A. C. 15, 17; A. J. 7; Anthony C. 1; James 1, 4; Joseph (black) 4; Mitchell 1; William 1, 2
TODD Eben 2
TOLLEY Traverse B. 5
TRAVERSE Arthur 3; Benjamin 1; Charles 1(twice), 5; George W. 1, 11, 12; J. Thomas 13; John W. (storekeeper) 1; Mary Ann 9; Prudence 4; Rosey 6; Samuel (of M.) 1; William D. 5
TRIGOE Job 17
TRIMBLE Samuel 12
TUBMAN Charles 10; Robert F. 12, 18
TULL Edward W. 5
TURPIN Francis B. C. 1; William 9
TWILLEY John W. 11; Samuel 1, 5
TYLER David W. 5

VANCE William J. 7
VICKARS Nathan 9
VICKERS & HANDLEY 7
VINCENT John 10

WAGGAMAN Eliza 14
WALLACE Anthony R. 18; James 2; 3(twice), 4, 8, 14, 19; James L., Sr 3
WAY The Reverend E. J. 3, 4
WEBB Josiah 11; Phany 9; Rickson (of Caroline County) 17
WELCH Robert Alexander 5
WHEATLEY Edward 1
WHEELER Peter 1; Sarah 13
WHITE & ANDERSON 7, 8, 12
WHITE Thomas 5, 11
WILCOX Henry 1, 8, 19
WILLEY Matthias 7
WILLIAMS (Also see CLIFT); Priscilla 18
WILLIS John 12; John L. 7
WILLSON Jacob 8
WILSON Jacob 19(twice); Susan 12
WINGATE Elizabeth 7; (Constable) George W. 6; Levin 5, 19
WOLFE Mrs. Jane (of Talbot County) 11
WOODARD Benjamin 10
WOODLAND Henry 7
WOODWIN Caleb 12
WOOLFORD Ellen 10; Hiram W. 1; John 10; Mary 5; Stevens B. 20; Thomas 20; W. 18; Whitefield 5, 10
WOOLLEA Levin 11
WRIGHT Ann Rebecca 20; Henry D. 17; Hester Ann 20; Isaac 18; Jeremiah 13; Jeremiah C. 12, 15; Mrs. Margaret W. 20; Martin L. 5; Mary E. 3
WRIGHTSON (Also see MUIR); Joshua 20
WROTEN Nancy 15
WROTTEN Daniel 4

YATES William H. 13

www.ingramcontent.com/pod-product-compliance
Lightning Source LLC
Chambersburg PA
CBHW080939030426

42339CB00009B/483